OUR GREAT STATES

WHAT'S GREAT ABOUT
ALASKA?

✳ Rebecca Felix

LERNER PUBLICATIONS ✳ MINNEAPOLIS

CONTENTS

ALASKA WELCOMES YOU! ✳ 4

Content Consultant: Jane Haigh, Assistant
Professor of History, Kenai Peninsula College

Lerner Publications Company
A division of Lerner Publishing Group, Inc.
241 First Avenue North
Minneapolis, MN 55401 USA

For reading levels and more information, look
up this title at www.lernerbooks.com.

Main body text set in ITC Franklin Gothic Std
Book Condensed 12/15.
Typeface provided by Adobe Systems.

Library of Congress Cataloging-in-Publication
Data

Felix, Rebecca, 1984–
       What's great about Alaska? / by
Rebecca Felix.
          pages cm. — (Our great states)
       Includes index.
       Audience: Grades 4–6.
       ISBN 978-1-4677-3888-0 (lb : alk.
paper) — ISBN 978-1-4677-8491-7 (pb :
alk. paper) — ISBN 978-1-4677-8492-4
(eb pdf)
       1. Alaska—Juvenile literature. I. Title.
F904.3.F47 2015
979.8—dc23   2015001940

Manufactured in the United States of America
1 - PC – 7/15/15

ALASKA Welcomes You!

Welcome to Alaska, a wild frontier of natural beauty! Alaska is twice as big as the next biggest US state. It is home to bears, wolves, moose, and more. How many animals will you see on your visit? Check out glaciers and snowy mountains as you hike, snowshoe, ski, or camp. You'll never forget Alaska's outdoor wonders! Try panning for gold in streams or racing through snow on sleds pulled by teams of dogs. Bundle up and get ready for adventure as you learn about ten things that make Alaska great!

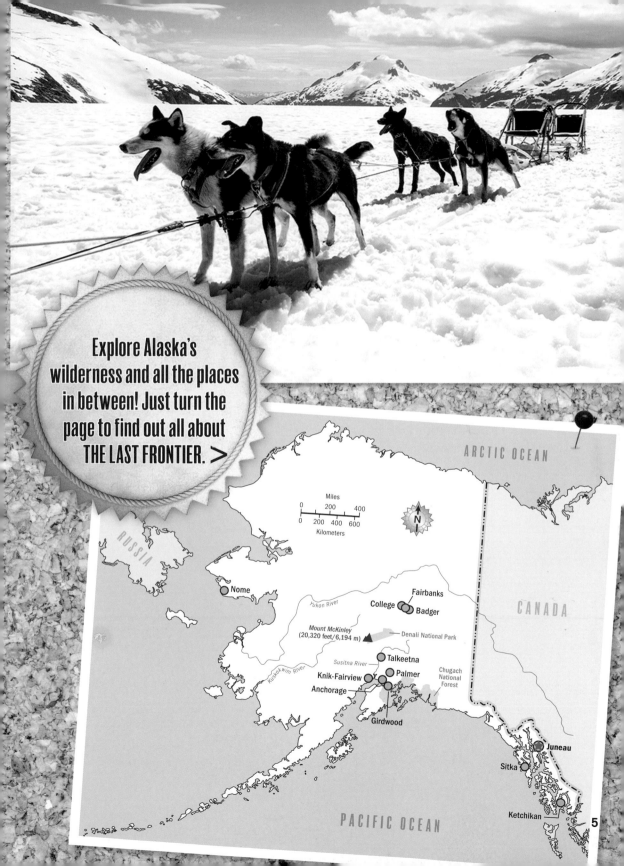

Explore Alaska's wilderness and all the places in between! Just turn the page to find out all about THE LAST FRONTIER. >

ARCTIC OCEAN

RUSSIA

CANADA

Miles
0   200   400
0   200 400 600
Kilometers

N

Nome

Yukon River

Fairbanks
College   Badger

Mount McKinley
(20,320 feet/6,194 m)   Denali National Park

Talkeetna
Susitna River
Knik-Fairview   Palmer   Chugach
National
Anchorage   Forest

Girdwood

Juneau

Sitka

Kuskokwim River

Ketchikan

PACIFIC OCEAN

GLACIER AND SEA LIFE ENCOUNTERS

Keep your eyes open for humpback and orca whales on your Whale Watch tour.

> Head out to sea in waters near Alaska. As your boat pushes its way past floating chunks of ice, you suddenly hear a loud crack! A chunk of ice from a glacier bigger than your boat crashes into the sea. Then there's another splash. You see a humpback whale break the surface of the water!

Alaska Tour Center's Juneau Whale Watch guarantees that you'll see whales on its half-day boat trip in the summer. You'll hear the whales' songs too. The boats have special equipment that picks up and plays whale calls from underwater. You might also see sea lions or black bears on your trip. Climb on Mendenhall Glacier at Tongass National Forest, where the tour makes a stop.

Get close to more icy glaciers with Alaska Travel Adventures. Its Glacier View Sea Kayaking is for adventurers ages seven and up. Settle into a kayak with an adult. Then follow a guide through the freezing sea. How many different animals do you see? The giant glaciers you pass might make you feel extra small!

GLACIERS

Some areas of Alaska are covered in snow all year. Glaciers are created when many layers of snow collect and turn to ice. New snow layers are added over hundreds of years. They flatten the ice until it becomes very dense. Geologists think most of Alaska was covered in glaciers millions of years ago. But glaciers have slowly been melting for thousands of years. As of 2013, they covered about 5 percent of the state.

ALASKA STATE FAIR

This huge cabbage won first place at the Alaska State Fair.

> Would you believe your eyes if you saw a carrot the size of a dog? Or a pumpkin bigger than you? See these sights and more at the Alaska State Fair in Palmer!

The fair is held at the end of each summer. This also marks the end of Alaska's unusual growing season. From June through August, the sun shines all day and nearly all night in parts of Alaska. Plants soak up the sun and just keep growing! People show off their monstrous fruits and vegetables at the fair for prizes. Past winners include a 20-pound (9-kilogram) carrot and a pumpkin that weighed more than 1,000 pounds (454 kg)!

Hundreds of thousands of people come to the fair to see more than 10,000 exhibits. Music stars perform concerts. There are circus and lumberjack shows and a carnival full of rides. Hop on the Ferris wheel for a good view of the Chugach Mountains. Meet robotic dinosaurs face to face at the fair. Watch the replicas move and roar. Some tower 9 feet (3 meters) tall! You can also see baby dinosaurs hatch and wiggle from eggs.

ALASKA'S MIDNIGHT SUN

Midnight sun happens near the north and south poles, where the sun is visible into the night. In some parts of Alaska, the sun shines day and night for more than two and a half months! In winter, there are weeks when the sun is never seen. This happens because of how Earth tilts. The north pole tilts toward the sun during summer. It is tilted away from the sun during the winter months.

DENALI NATIONAL PARK

> Denali National Park covers more than 6 million acres (2.4 million hectares) in Alaska. Tundra, forest, and snow-covered mountains fill the park. Mount McKinley is located there. It is the highest mountain in North America.

Once you arrive at Denali National Park, hop on a shuttle bus. It will drive you through the park. Your challenge on the bus is to spot the Denali Big Five. These are the five largest animals in the park. They are caribou, Dall sheep, grizzly bears, moose, and wolves.

You can see more of the landscape on a snowshoe or cross-country ski tour. For faster exploration of the park, take an all-terrain vehicle (ATV) tour. Hold on tight as your driver climbs steep mountainsides and speeds through open tundra.

Want to take your time exploring? Try a ranger-led hike. Then make your way to the Murie Science and Learning Center. It offers youth camping in the park. Who knows? You might spot the Big Five right outside your tent!

If you're lucky, you may see a moose and her calves at Denali National Park.

Explore the park on a snowshoe hike with a park ranger.

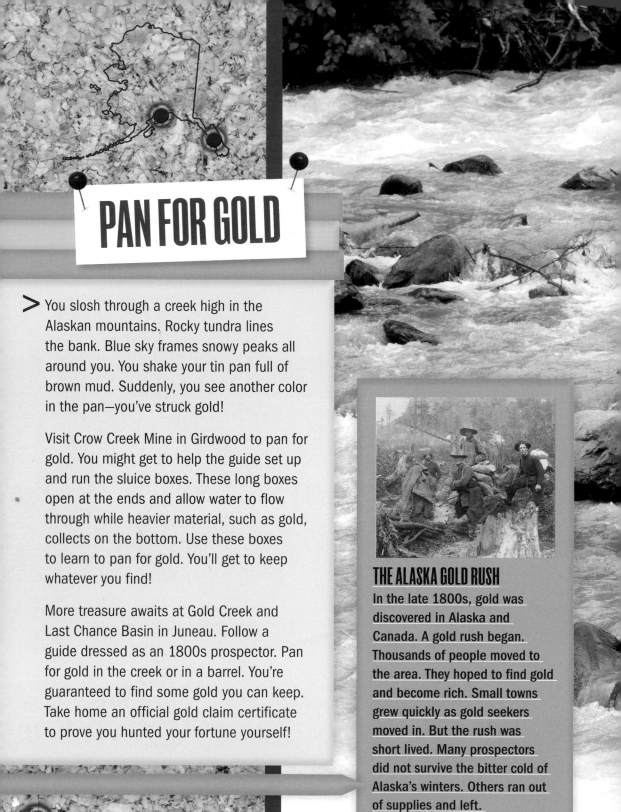

PAN FOR GOLD

> You slosh through a creek high in the Alaskan mountains. Rocky tundra lines the bank. Blue sky frames snowy peaks all around you. You shake your tin pan full of brown mud. Suddenly, you see another color in the pan—you've struck gold!

Visit Crow Creek Mine in Girdwood to pan for gold. You might get to help the guide set up and run the sluice boxes. These long boxes open at the ends and allow water to flow through while heavier material, such as gold, collects on the bottom. Use these boxes to learn to pan for gold. You'll get to keep whatever you find!

More treasure awaits at Gold Creek and Last Chance Basin in Juneau. Follow a guide dressed as an 1800s prospector. Pan for gold in the creek or in a barrel. You're guaranteed to find some gold you can keep. Take home an official gold claim certificate to prove you hunted your fortune yourself!

THE ALASKA GOLD RUSH

In the late 1800s, gold was discovered in Alaska and Canada. A gold rush began. Thousands of people moved to the area. They hoped to find gold and become rich. Small towns grew quickly as gold seekers moved in. But the rush was short lived. Many prospectors did not survive the bitter cold of Alaska's winters. Others ran out of supplies and left.

Visit historic gold mining buildings at Crow Creek Mine.

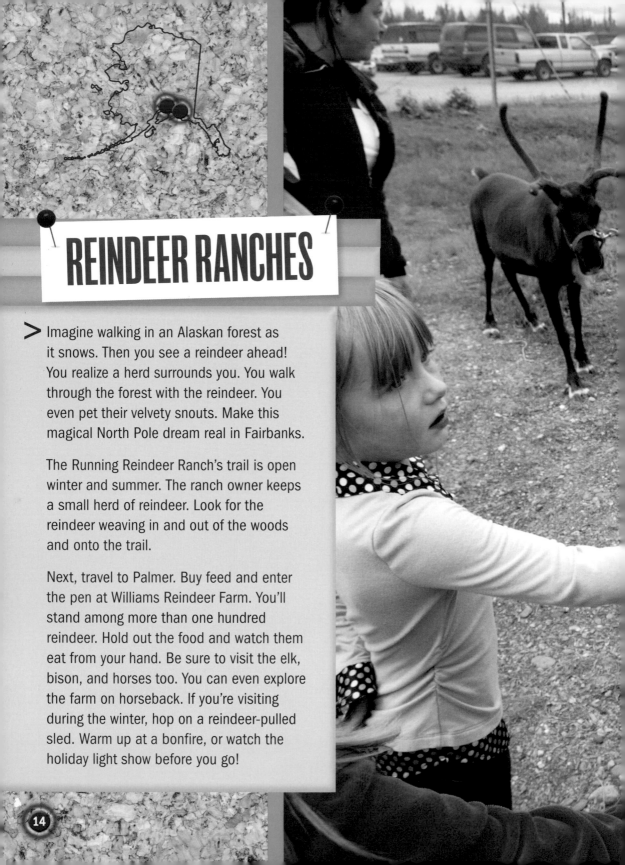

REINDEER RANCHES

> Imagine walking in an Alaskan forest as it snows. Then you see a reindeer ahead! You realize a herd surrounds you. You walk through the forest with the reindeer. You even pet their velvety snouts. Make this magical North Pole dream real in Fairbanks.

The Running Reindeer Ranch's trail is open winter and summer. The ranch owner keeps a small herd of reindeer. Look for the reindeer weaving in and out of the woods and onto the trail.

Next, travel to Palmer. Buy feed and enter the pen at Williams Reindeer Farm. You'll stand among more than one hundred reindeer. Hold out the food and watch them eat from your hand. Be sure to visit the elk, bison, and horses too. You can even explore the farm on horseback. If you're visiting during the winter, hop on a reindeer-pulled sled. Warm up at a bonfire, or watch the holiday light show before you go!

At the end of your tour at Running Reindeer Ranch, pet the reindeer's thick fur and fuzzy antlers.

Enjoy a snack of hot chocolate and cookies at Running Reindeer Ranch.

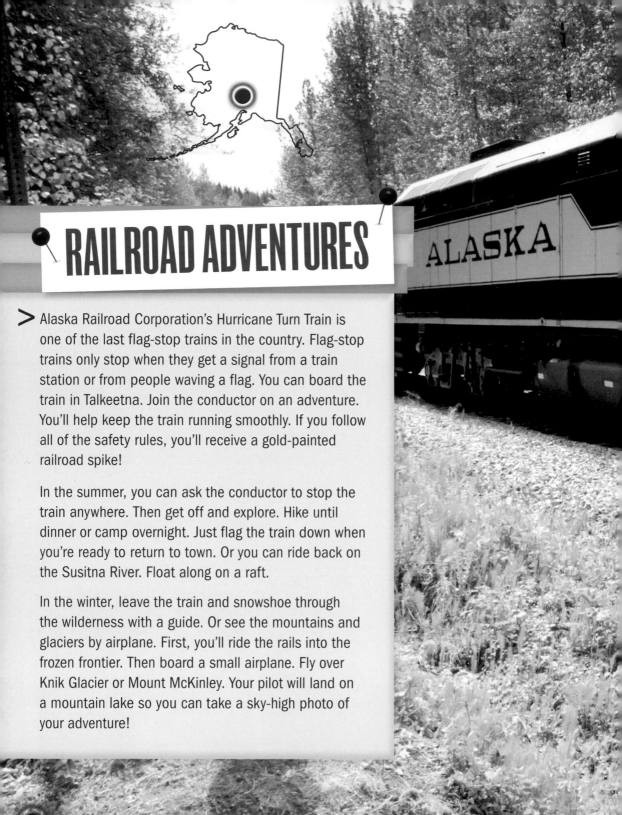

RAILROAD ADVENTURES

> Alaska Railroad Corporation's Hurricane Turn Train is one of the last flag-stop trains in the country. Flag-stop trains only stop when they get a signal from a train station or from people waving a flag. You can board the train in Talkeetna. Join the conductor on an adventure. You'll help keep the train running smoothly. If you follow all of the safety rules, you'll receive a gold-painted railroad spike!

In the summer, you can ask the conductor to stop the train anywhere. Then get off and explore. Hike until dinner or camp overnight. Just flag the train down when you're ready to return to town. Or you can ride back on the Susitna River. Float along on a raft.

In the winter, leave the train and snowshoe through the wilderness with a guide. Or see the mountains and glaciers by airplane. First, you'll ride the rails into the frozen frontier. Then board a small airplane. Fly over Knik Glacier or Mount McKinley. Your pilot will land on a mountain lake so you can take a sky-high photo of your adventure!

Look for wildlife along the Susitna River.

You'll see great views of Alaska from the air on an airplane ride!

17

FUR RENDEZVOUS

> Would you ride an outdoor Ferris wheel in winter? Or run a race through snow? You can if you visit Alaska during the Fur Rendezvous! It is a winter festival held in Anchorage each year. Some people call it the "World's Coldest, Craziest Winter Carnival."

Kick off the fest by running in the Frostbite Footrace and Costume Fun Run. People wear funny costumes—make sure yours is warm! Another popular race is the Running of the Reindeer. Watch adults try to outrun real reindeer! People also race downhill on outhouses placed atop skis. And softball players try to run around the bases in snowshoes during snowy outdoor softball games.

At night watch figure skaters spin and twirl, or see Alaska's top snowboarders flip and fly as fireworks light up the sky. Become a winter athlete yourself with ice bowling or ice skating. Help bounce others into the sky at the Blanket Toss, an Eskimo tradition. Climb onto the blanket yourself, and a crowd of people will send you flying!

The Blanket Toss is a favorite event during the Fur Rendezvous.

Cheer on the softball players as they play a game while wearing snowshoes.

DOGSLEDDING

Meet and pet the Alaska Excursion dogs that pull your sled.

> A team of huskies kicks up snow as they race past mountains. They twist and turn at top speed, looking like a streak of fur. You're tucked inside the sled they pull! Salmon Berry Tours dogsled adventures go through Chugach State Park. The tours include a break to explore the woods by snowshoe. At a trailside stop, warm up at a fire and have s'mores.

Dogsledding doesn't stop when summer arrives. Alaska Excursions offers summer adventures with dogs. Ride a special ATV up a mountain in Tongass National Forest. Meet a musher and a team of excited huskies at the top. Jump on the wheeled sled and hold on. The dogs will pull you down the mountainside! At the end, ask professional mushers questions. Learn about the dogs or the Iditarod, a world-famous dogsled race. Or cuddle fluffy sled dog puppies in training while sitting around a bonfire.

IDITAROD TRAIL SLED DOG RACE

The Iditarod is the most famous dogsledding race in the world. It has been held in Alaska for more than forty years. Each March, mushers race more than 1,000 miles (1,609 kilometers) between Anchorage and Nome. Teams cross frozen waterways and mountain ranges. They camp in snow and ice for a minimum of ten days. Veterinarians and officials make sure the dogs are healthy and safe during the long race.

TRIBAL TOURS

> Have you ever stood in a forest of totem poles? Have you danced with Eskimo dancers to the beat of traditional drums? You can do both in Alaska! Watch lively dancers perform on the Saxman Native Village Tour in Ketchikan. Study their moves. Then join them for the final dance! To cool down after your dance, head outside to Totem Bight State Historical Park. Stare up in awe at one of the biggest collections of totem poles in the world. See how they're made at the Village Carving Center. Watch young carvers learning to create the huge works of art.

You can also see totem poles at Alaska Native Heritage Center in Anchorage. Giant whale bones rest on its grounds. Whales and whale hunting are important in some Inupiat cultures. Stand underneath a bone arch outside the center's tribal villages. Each of the six villages has traditional Eskimo dwellings. You can meet tribal members and listen to their stories as you examine and try out authentic games, tools, and utensils.

ALASKA'S NATIVE CULTURES

Alaska is home to many groups of indigenous people. Some of these include the Aleut, Inupiat, Yupik, and Athabascans. At least twenty languages are spoken in Alaska. Indigenous people made up approximately 16 percent of the state's population in 2013.

How many totem poles can you find at Totem Bight State Historical Park?

WORLD ICE ART CHAMPIONSHIPS

> Zip down an icy slide hundreds of feet long. Zigzag through a glowing, rainbow-colored ice maze at night. See an ice tiger as big as a car or a clear castle glitter in the sun. These sights are in Fairbanks each winter!

The World Ice Art Championships last more than one month. Teams from around the world carve blocks of ice into giant works of art. Two beautiful examples include a huge bird inside a delicate icicle cage and a dragon breathing swirling streams of icy fire. In daylight, sunshine lights up the sculptures like glittering crystal. At night, bright, colorful lights shine from within.

The festival's ice-skating rink, bordered by ice walls, also glows with lights. So does a massive ice maze in Kids Park. There are 16 ice slides, some more than 200 feet (61 m) long in the park. And don't miss riding the Twirlies. These spinning ice sculptures are shaped like balls or teardrops. Curl up inside or sit atop one. Have someone else spin and swirl the Twirly as you hold on tight!

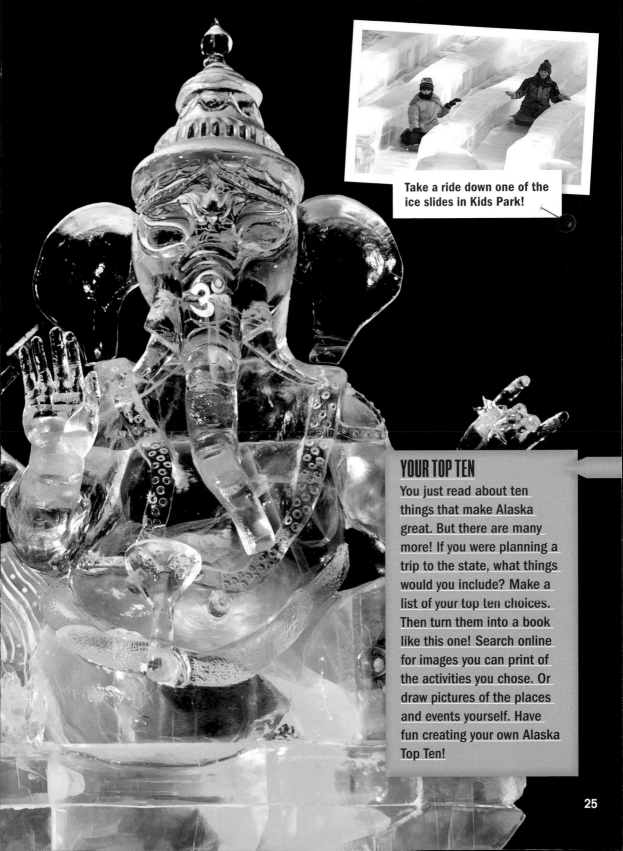

Take a ride down one of the ice slides in Kids Park!

YOUR TOP TEN

You just read about ten things that make Alaska great. But there are many more! If you were planning a trip to the state, what things would you include? Make a list of your top ten choices. Then turn them into a book like this one! Search online for images you can print of the activities you chose. Or draw pictures of the places and events yourself. Have fun creating your own Alaska Top Ten!

ALASKA BY MAP

> MAP KEY

- Capital city
- City
- Point of interest
- Highest elevation
- --·-- International border

RUSSIA

Visit www.lerneresource.com to learn more about the state flag of Alaska.

ARCTIC OCEAN

CANADA

Miles
0   200   400
0   200 400 600
Kilometers

N

Running Reindeer Ranch

World Ice Art Championship

Murie Science and Learning Center

Nome

Yukon River

College   Badger

Fairbanks

Mount McKinley
(20,320 feet/6,194 m)

Denali National Park

Susitna River

Hurricane Turn Train

Talkeetna

Kuskokwim River

Knik-Fairview

Anchorage

Palmer

Alaska State Fair

Williams Reindeer Farm

Chugach National Forest

Fur Rendezvous

Girdwood

Crow Creek Mine

Mendenhall Glacier

Juneau

Sitka

Ketchikan

PACIFIC OCEAN

ALASKA FACTS

NICKNAME: The Last Frontier

SONG: "Alaska's Flag" by Marie Drake

MOTTO: "North to the Future"

> FLOWER: alpine forget-me-not

TREE: Sitka spruce

BIRD: willow ptarmigan

> ANIMAL: moose

DATE AND RANK OF STATEHOOD: January 3, 1959; 49th state

> CAPITAL: Juneau

AREA: 590,693 square miles (1,529,888 sq. km)

AVERAGE JANUARY TEMPERATURE: 5°F (-15°C)

AVERAGE JULY TEMPERATURE: 55°F (13°C)

POPULATION AND RANK: 735,132; 47th (2013)

MAJOR CITIES AND POPULATIONS: Anchorage (300,950), Juneau (32,660), Fairbanks (32,324), Badger (19,482), Sitka (9,020)

NUMBER OF US CONGRESS MEMBERS: 1 representative, 2 senators

NUMBER OF ELECTORAL VOTES: 3

> NATURAL RESOURCES: copper, fish, gold, natural gas, oil, soil, zinc

AGRICULTURAL PRODUCTS: barley, hay, hogs, oats, potatoes, reindeer, sheep

MANUFACTURED GOODS: petroleum products

STATE HOLIDAYS AND CELEBRATIONS: Alaska Day, Alaska State Fair, Seward's Day

GLOSSARY

conductor: a person who collects tickets on a train

frontier: a place where few people live and where there is much wilderness to explore

glacier: a slow-moving mass made of ice found in polar regions

indigenous: originally living in a certain area

musher: a person who drives a sled dog team

prospector: a person who explores in search of gold or silver

replica: an exact copy of something, often made smaller in size

totem pole: a wooden pole carved by native peoples of the Northwest Coast, showing animals, plants, and other objects to represent family tribal symbols

tundra: frozen ground covered by low-growing plants and no trees

LERNER

SOURCE™

Expand learning beyond the printed book. Download free, complementary educational resources for this book from our website, www.lerneresource.com.

FURTHER INFORMATION

Alaska Kids
www.alaskakids.org
Find photos and information about Alaska's animals, a cool cartoon about Alaska's native cultures, online games, quick facts, and a huge list of books about the state!

Alaska.org: How Big Is Alaska?
www.alaska.org/how-big-is-alaska
Select any US state from a drop-down menu, and see its outline placed inside an outline of Alaska to compare the state's two sizes!

Daly, Ruth. *Denali*. New York: AV2 by Weigl, 2013. Read all about Denali National Park and North America's highest peak, Mount McKinley. Find out what animals live there, along with legends people have created about the massive mountain.

Gill, Shelley. *Alaska*. Watertown, MA: Charlesbridge, 2007. Read about Alaska's animals, volcanoes, dogsledding, people, and geography. The book is written by a state resident and explorer.

Orr, Tamra B. *Alaska*. New York: Children's Press, 2014. Find colorful photographs and fun facts about Alaska's people, government, land, and history.

State of Alaska: Alaska Kids' Corner
alaska.gov/kids
Learn more about Alaska with facts, maps, and articles. Find tons of links on history, outdoor activities, animals, and frequently asked questions about the state.

INDEX

PHOTO ACKNOWLEDGMENTS

The images in this book are used with the permission of: © Ruth Peterkin/Shutterstock Images, p. 1; NASA, pp. 2–3; © Laura Westlund/Independent Picture Service, pp. 5 (bottom), 27; © Purestock/Thinkstock, p. 4; © ad foto/iStockphoto, p. 5 (top); © Karl Weatherly/Photodisc/Thinkstock, pp. 6–7; © Wildnerdpix/Shutterstock Images, p. 7; © Luke Jones CC 2.0, pp. 8–9; © Clark James Mishler/Design Pics Inc./Alamy, p. 8 (top); © Christopher Boswell/Shutterstock Images, p. 8 (bottom); © Jacob W. Frank/US National Park Service, pp. 10–11, 11 (left); © Daniel A. Leifheit/US National Park Service, p. 11 (right); © Doug Lindstrand/Design Pics Inc./Alamy, pp. 12–13; © Clark James Mishler/ZumaPress/Newscom, p. 13; Library of Congress, pp. 12 (LC-USZ62-103287), 22 (LC-USZ62-48116); © Fairbanks Daily News-Miner/ZumaPress/Newscom, pp. 14–15; © mb-fotos/iStockphoto, p. 15 (top); © B. and E. Dudzinscy/Shutterstock Images, p. 15 (bottom); © David L. Moore - AK/Alamy, pp. 16–17; © dolka82/Shutterstock Images, p. 17 (top); © Richard A McMillin/Shutterstock Images, p. 17 (bottom); © Al Grillo/ZumaPress/Newscom, pp. 18–19; © Accent Alaska.com/Alamy, pp. 19 (top), 22–23; © WorldFoto/Alamy, p. 19 (bottom); © Andreea Dragomir/Shutterstock Images, pp. 20–21; © Robin Keefe/Shutterstock Images, p. 20; © mdcooper/iStockphoto, p. 21; © alysta/Shutterstock Images, p. 23; © Gary Whitton/Shutterstock Images, pp. 24–25; © Jay Cross CC 2.0, p. 24; © Eric Engman/ZumaPress/Newscom, p. 25; © nicoolay/iStockphoto, p. 26; © Tom Grundy/Shutterstock Images, p. 29 (top); © Photography by J.H. Williams/iStockphoto, p. 29 (middle left); © B. Calkins/Shutterstock Images, p. 29 (middle right); © optimarc/Shutterstock Images, p. 29 (bottom).

Cover: © Alaska Photography/Getty Images (dogsledding); © iStockphoto.com/Nancy Nehring (totem pole); © iStockphoto.com/webguzs (bear); © Laura Westlund/Independent Picture Service (map); © iStockphoto.com/fpm (seal); © iStockphoto.com/vicm (pushpins); © iStockphoto.com/benz190 (cork board).